NOCTIS LICENTIA

NOCTIS LICENTIA

Amy Lawless

Black Maze Books, New York

Published by Black Maze Books, New York.

www.blackmazebooks.com

Published in the USA.

ISBN 978-0-6152-0272-3

Cover Design: Alex Smith.

TABLE OF CONTENTS

I

II

III

for PCC

NOCTIS LICENTIA

"What is done out of love always takes place beyond good and evil."

FRIEDRICH NIETZSCHE

"Our virtues and our failings are inseparable, like force and matter. When they separate, man is no more."

NIKOLA TESLA

"Hell, there are no rules here — we're trying to accomplish something."

THOMAS A. EDISON

I

Selections From *Top One Thousand Insect Tragedies*

At the old age of four, Brigitte, a Chicago bedbug, died alone on a crackhead's mattress miles from her nearest relative.

Charles, a Palmetto bug from Tallahassee, Fla., was crushed when a woman closed her cabinet door onto him.

Equitable beetle from Toronto, Hal, was insecticided.

Unable to rub his legs together to make his song a depressed Jean-Louis, a Haitian cricket, threw himself in front of a truck.

John, a fire ant from a large suburban family, was stepped on by a thirteen year-old on a tennis court.

Tina Rodriguez, a ladybug, was trapped inside a piece of luggage on United Flight 175 on September 11, 2001.

Paul, the first moth in his family to step foot inside a college, was trapped unceremoniously between a screen and a window frame and starved to death in October. His wife witnessed the whole thing but was unable to push food through the screen due to her ceaseless histrionics.

A free-loving flea named Harold jumped up the nose of a tourist at the Louvre. He was blown out dead a few minutes later.

After a fight with his mate, Gene "Sully" Sullivan, a Bostonian fly, stormed off into the wrong arlirshaft at a local university and was never seen or heard from again.

Ben, a cockroach living in the Lower East Side of Manhattan, got caught in a sticky mousetrap. Two of his children watched him try to escape the ooze for an hour before he told them to retreat to the nest. They thankfully didn't witness Karen Ng crush him with a small brown bag hours later.

Elvis Ender, drifter aphid, wandered onto an electric chair moments before a convicted murderer was executed in Texas on August 18, 2006.

Jeff "Scooter" Hamlin, a firefly from Arlington, Virginia, was kidnapped by the McKinley twins and suffocated to death in a mason jar.

After a small kitten batted off Craig Schloss' sixth leg, he hobbled into some tall grass and starved. The same kitten ate his body two days later.

Local honeybee Zelda Smith got too close to the Barber family's ceiling fan. As it was oscillating on high, it clipped off her wings and she fell 10 feet to her death. She was unconscious upon impact and felt nothing.

Carol and Jim Glendale, two middle-aged butterflies looking to spice up their sex life, were making love in the air. They smashed into the windshield of a Dodge minivan and were wiped off cleanly.

Single mother of two hundred Bertie Jenkins died when a fire engulfed the nest she and her children lived in.

While sucking a bloodfeast from the body of actor Charlton Heston, California mosquito Jenny Wong suffered a cardiac arrest.

After mating a stunningly gorgeous female mantis named Julia, Matthew McDonald was eaten limb by limb. His last words were "*Non, je ne regrette rien.*"

SONNET

You're a busy beetle on its back,
I hold the stock over the rest of your day.
Should I flip you or allow you to decay?
I glare at the crow on the wire, keeping it at bay.
Its beak a skewer, the leaf you lie on a tray.
For breakfast you ate a little grub.
For lunch you began a stem to nub.

Never one for violence, but always one for shame,
I let you writtle there indebted to my name.
I tickle your exo, finger your antennae,
I consider licking your shell as part of the game.
But I flip you back over, and you scuttle away.
You've had enough of this game for the day.
The crow is still hungry, and hungry he'll stay.

OH FLESH!

When a life has just expired
And the smell of trauma lifts
Into the air where I have spiraled
And lean my wings toward your new gifts

My head looks like it'd gobble, gobble—
But to feast on this terminated tissue
My feathery face simply won't do!

To bathe my mind in the carcass,
To turn my beak crimson,
To make the bones break
And to eat out your ear
A face that looks like raw meat itself
Red and wrinkly, hairless too,
Lets the soul reach out and say

"Oh flesh!"

FLAMING O

You are a monster made of pencils
walking on a dry-erase board,
holding yourself impossibly up,
joined at the sharpened tips.
Your jaw clatters like lead.
You spat like a vintage pen,
squirting your stuffs at me.
And only then did I see
you were waving your flaming asshole at me.
Feathers flutter.
I guess your O is pretty enough for me
to approach.
Raise your wings.
Yes, like that.

EXUBERANCE

It took hours to get into Franklin Park

Hundreds of mammals wait in line to see more mammals

But I stroll to the busy peacocks plumes always in bloom

To the courtyard where the sun tears through the trees confidently

The zookeeper holds a hose spraying the boycocks and girlcocks just for fun

Drenching my hair before he even recognizes me

Among the other physiologically exuberant birds

My Edge Of Country

I rub up against coasts.
Coasts sing so sweet back to me
Lining my back with rocks, earthworks,
Crumbled stone and sand for my head to rest on,
A warm spring to dip my feet in—therapeutic.
Dipped into
Sensations dropping and halving themselves into
Factions.
Little elves, little booties, little religions.

Candle wax dripping down elevator shafts,
We found a place to waltz
Into each other as long as it's a dark hole.
Mining, diving, controlling my dreams to
fly.

Not everyone has to divide his manhood from his clover.

CALLING IN

after Li Po's Sick Leave

In bed, avoiding the daily grind
All week away from mirrors and from doors
I continue to disbelieve I'm the man in the elliptical room
It started by jerking myself off to sleep until I became sick
Peace can bloom in matchbox or in shoe
I lie in a room three coffins wide and long
From the window outside my bed is the monument against the sky
A cloud covers the tip like a bonnet
Dishonoring the men under the earth

SUPER DESTINY

I am not patching up lies about desire
Or rubbing my legs together to create fire.
Nothing touches me in this mirror-lined box.
My blue eyes are bigger than my heart, and your cocks.
I sit on these moos and meows, shamefully tossed.
But view me in Technicolor with your eyes crossed.
Stomach bulges are only for forgetting.
I will be wearing a clean-slated golden ring
And some rosemary, my kryptonite other.
I'll be a cripple, but so is every mother.

JUNE IN AUTUMN

Herr: Es ist Zeit. Der Sommer war sehr groß.

Sir, it's time. The grand time for the absurd.
Deposed hombres have changed from sullen to merry—
Free to ravish and soothe the little piano ladies.

During the fourth note, he anchors his column to her extreme fruits;
She concedes to his anchor, providing he keeps the tempo.
His fruits join hers until they both reach maturity. Hell, it's spring!
Not like that sad wine they sip in distant autumns.

She is not ravaged on some over-priced furniture, nor left for later.
She alone is lunged alone. He spit out his frog on her.
Screw it, let me be plain: she is on fire and not sullen and he is a living tornado.
Peaceful in the void, he farts the frog aria.

NEW YORK IN WINTER

Darling, would you hold this light string
As I untangle it for the Christmas tree? Frost
Has begun forming on the sills again. I lost
The fuse just like last year. The thing

Is that these people should be humbled
To be invited to such a grandiose place
As ours! We act like a gingerbread house assembled
With all these cakes, lights, icings! I hate hosting our open house!

Even though you always say, "It's just one night
Out of the whole year!" Those people live on farms!
Jeez! And they show up in overalls, pouring out of a van.
Darl, don't you realize that I am just one man
I don't always think I'm better than them but in this case I'm right...
Don't leave! I'll never untangle these lights with just my arms.

GIRL TALK

I said "Oh hon, you'll find your place
Among the stinking stagnant human grime."

I poured some tea and sat—just her and me—
And listened to the endless parade of dates
That each commenced far too late
And ended very early the next day.

If ever I did wonder why she kept
Putting herself out there into the mix
I only had to look back at myself
And my most perfect life to see
That we are all here to accumulate
A perfect love and once we have,
Settle into mediocrity.

And then I got a brilliant clue
Of how I could make her feel much less blue.
I told her that her fire still did burn
And showed her the huge circumference of my thigh,
How I was slowly melting to the chair.

And then I turned the baby monitor up to ten
So she could hear the wailing of my spawn.
She smiled and her eye avoided mine
The joy of the chase lifted her from the chair
And she got the hell out of here.

Her French Is Incredible

Her French is incredible.
How does she know it?
She read the menu in this voice every night
Ignoring my question, "How did you get to Montreal?"
And asked for the pregnancy test in an accent that made my skin melt.
It was *très*.

Then, when it was time to have a conversation about what to do with *lui*,
She kept talking in French and more French.
Her words got faster.
And more French.
I said, "Can you translate?"
Non non non
I said, "Abortion clinic"
And she understood that shit quite well.
She walked away god I love that ass.

A REACTION TO NOTHING HAPPENING

We didn't meet at the appointed time
As no time was appointed.
The pipe that works like a radiator blazes for the first time today.

We've never even met.
We did meet in my head.
We were both wearing bumblebee-striped sweaters we gave each other
For our fourth Christmas together.
I looked you in the eyes
And thought you fat son of a bitch what happened?

You're Amazing And I Love You

Fortune is a spinning record player, overpriced pills, and 16 grapefruits.
Ugly cousins and ghostwriters don't mentor like you.
Can't you understand cigarette holder words?
Knights and dangerous lawyers—we defy them all.

Your cattle, splayed with a mace, my bed, a bull's eyed waste.
Oh that sound is just my hat. Let's weave a flag together for our team.
Underneath all my frilly clothes are the cleanest-shaven legs.

GLAD TO HEAR IT'S SUCH A GOOD SANDWICH

Glad to hear it's such a good sandwich
I personally don't have enough money for one
You'd give me a bite if you weren't such a bitch

The mayonnaise is particularly rich?
Is there any way I could convince you to lend me money, hon?
Glad to hear it's such a good sandwich

You're right, the décor in here is seventies kitsch
They don't take credit cards. Could you make a bank run?
You'd give me a bite if you weren't such a bitch

I'm starting to feel my stomach pitch
There's a bit of turkey on your lip. You're clearly having fun
Glad to hear it's such a good sandwich

If I can't try it, I'll throw myself into a ditch,
Die of hunger and decay into a skeleton
You'd give me a bite if you weren't such a bitch

Never have I met such a dead-on witch
You know how I adore a Portuguese bun.
Glad to hear it's such a good sandwich
You'd give me a bite if you weren't such a bitch.

CORRESPONDENCE

Like the moment the Christmas tree lights go on
and the furthest person from your thoughts is
Baby Jesus. Distracted by bugs in the light fixtures.
Distracted by chirping cockroaches in the hallway.
He keeps tabs on my comings and goings.
Dancing. Sniff my pits. Sniff your pits? Sniff them.
We each told our own lessons, our creation myths.
My barbies having sex. The dictionary for penis.
Wikipedia for masturbation. I love it when you
read to me. They left before the *I Have a Dream*
speech. I can say *llll* and I can say *of*. But I can't
put the sounds together.

Like the moment I was battered by endorphins,
baked by the boring repetition of your touch. Gifted,
we fell in love. Gifted love notes never existed
and she stopped believing in love. Remember how
she can't even say it. Or repeat on high, retard.

I know a great man with a disease and a wedding ring.
He does not drug me and therefore I do not read his
poetry. It should not surprise you that we are not in love
and that I am not married to him. We don't even ride
the same train. But our stories happen on the same leaf.
A fiberless cloud hangs in the sky. Just keep going
until five o'clock. Then come home and take care of business.

GLACIER BOXING

When I licked your icy wall—home
A place to fight
When I think before this time,
I sweat instead of breathe
Your light little ankles
Are the twitch in my eye
(Can I lean here?)
Tired in the fifth round,
We hug hard
And transfuse
True love waits without the ring
On mornings, noon, and sometimes nights
Keep the heart unclogged down and right
The gold around his waist,
The redness on his face,
A boxer off the screen
I battle him unseen

INTERNET HISTORY DECEMBER 7, 2006

Last day

BACK

HOME

Regret drinking too much wine last night
Swallow antibiotic
Bronchitis cough
Nothing is curing asthma
Inhaled steroids for women/fear of chest hair?
Choose an outfit when I hate all clothing
Marijuana OK for people with asthma?
Liquid soap versus bar soap
Face soap for sensitive skin, cost benefit analysis
Using the same towel for three days in a row
Listerine Whitening
Listerine Whitening: remember e-mail from mom said don't use
Homebrewed roasted coffee
One-a-Day Women's Vitamin
Not telling ex-boyfriend who I thought about when we fucked
The entire Boston Celtics team (African American members only)
Tropicana Orange Juice is overpriced
Mixing vanilla yogurt with granola
Low carb diets worth it? No.
Wiping sunscreen/moisturizer on face, I am a shiny beastess
XXX AARID Deodorant, powder fresh
Splenda was discovered in a lab researching poisons, pour packet into coffee
Bipolar men, poison sugar
Skim milk
Remembering making out with someone I never made out with
Stir the devil I know
Not the *New York Times* but favored
A picture of Britney Spears' cleavage, my cleavage last Friday night, a
    comparison thereof

Remembering to bring a box of raisins to work
1 train, coffin ride
ConEd Ad with Danny DeVito look-alike saying "I'm ON it."
Deciding not to let DeVito get on my it
Finding a dollar in wallet behind hate notes
Buying the cheap coffee from man in a metal box who always smiles and is nice
Men comment on my nice ass
Smile through the hating it
Three hours editing passages about John Steinbeck
Comparisons flaccid
Steinbeck not flaccid
Marijuana OK for asthmatics.
Walking by the church and remember how I cried in front of it on Valentine's
    Day and called
ex-boyfriend in front of church telling him I was lonely
A salad with ingredients = mathematical equation adding up to not hating
    my thighs
another day
Wondering if I am still lonely
Having these thighs but loving my ass
John Steinbeck's story called Breakfast
Wikipedia the meal *breakfast* by accident: fascinating read
There's always love in a Bee-Gee's song
Bipolar men?: worth it?
Steinbeck became really annoying & preachy later in his life
Steinbeck was lonely but for his dog
Not thinking about the Steinbeck when the Mozart comes on the IPOD
Dog in NYC?
Walking home push through strangers, gay gay Chelsea
Decaying New York
The man who broke his leg falling through the street grate
Avoiding street grates
Grabbing an elbow, but it's mine

Slice of pizza
Dust off feet
Raking ears, metal crash
Clutch keys
Slice of pizza realized
Switch shampoos?
Bipolar men: the devil I know
Those men in suits coming home from *Ernst & Young*—too boring?
The *New York Times*
A movie I've watched a hundred times: *The Big Lebowski*
Exiled like Li Po and Pound
Good to have a day without wine
Another shower this time clean
Opening an Oreo Cookie
Looks like the moon so I eat it.
Don't forget to brush teeth
Second Oreo Cookie
Brush Teeth
Listerine Whitening, why?
Time for sleep

MAKING A KILLING

The dime-sized nostrils on the manchild.
A guilty conscience shows through my purple nail polish.
Old boyfriends, old bedrooms, old secretaries of defense.
New boyfriends, smaller bedrooms, the queen of offense.

Making a phone with my hand, calling you across the room.
"Hello, my best friend has to go into the Israeli army so I'm not doing you
    tonight."
I wake up and he's dead! I wake up and he is alive. I wake up and I'm you.
I wake up next to you.

My art is just putting a leather jacket on a blank canvas and hanging it to
    the wall.
Applause for originality. Applause.
Pull my hand through my hair in nervous vanity.

CRY WOLF (BRIEF MOMENTS IN NULL-MEXICO)

Dien perceives my B.A.C.,
serves me club soda and snails.
A realtor wearing a headset
eats *Filet-O-Fish*, places a finger into my butt-crack.
Some do coke. Others talk about
how they don't do coke, then fuck the people who do coke.
And the whole time,
my tampon disrobes
in my purse, begging entry.
Oh agent provocateur,
I can't stand all this honesty down south!

THE VIRGIN QUEEN

I went inside Queen Elizabeth I's shriveled head
to check out the new transportation
museum's cocktail party. It ended up being kind of boring
and to get out I had to take an elevator

with all these pregnant women and a pregnant
Sri Lankan man with a cane. Thought I
wasn't pregnant and that maybe I didn't belong
in that elevator. But we all belong in that

elevator. All us typists in a lifeboat,
Billy goats sneaking past avoiding contact,
smacking lasagna hogs. Sneak past Queen
Victoria's boat-sized body. Two child laborers crafting

velvets to cover up her corpse's sausage stench.
They're little silkworms pissing
the string and knitting it up with little
hands, their small tired hands.

Let me escape great Queens. Let me
clean out this Grand Central Station nightmare,
which starts where it ends: England,
coloring the basin of my shower with vomit,
miles from home.

CLOSE, CLOSER, CLOSEST

A hooded figure in the window
Framed like a medieval painting
Robed in a scarlet robbed from that age.

Her head bobs due to the hacking coughs
That plagued everyone those days, or so we've heard.

She is a woman with the shoulders of a hunchback in her bell tower.
Ignore her.
It's not a cough but how she moves her shoulders
when she pulls at her lip like it is a panty elastic for snapping.
Nervous habit for a shut-in.

Glad to hear I'm being talked about in the third person.
Let's just agree I'm aloof and some fancy word I haven't found yet while
    picking my lip
and staring over the dictionary unsatisfied with being obtuse in my bell tower.
You're prejudiced against asthmatics.
I have a hunch that you have your own bell towers too.

Alpha empty face. Left eye cries Andre. Right eye cries Andre. No spirit or energy—but Andre. Wandering, plucking my lashes, watering my daisy. Andre won't leave. I never met Andre. Leaning on my elbow until it turns face Andre red. I have not met Andre. Don't know if I'll ever meet Andre and his hilarious chorus of large black women. You've never met Andre. You've talked to him on the phone many times. THESE CONVERSATIONS HAVE LASTED FOR HOURS. He knows what I'm talking about. Andre. We need to meet Andre. We could never meet Andre. He is powerful. Andre wants to meet us. I'm almost asleep with Andre. Tell him. Tell him we're fine. We're going to his house, Andre. He lives just a few blocks away. Andre has taken it all. He has taken all the land. Andre owns everything. Andre the pillager of villages and rapist of thankful women. Andre the watcher. Believe Andre. He has watched you fuck. He has watched me fuck. Leaning on Andre will cause twelve thousand orgasms. His face is red. He has mowed many, many lawns. Andre has moved many cars. He plays poker. When we parallel park well, we park like Andre. Andre: the Word template for any document you want to write. Andre: the author and star of *The Dictionary of a Hero*, the *Lives of a Saint*. Andre, whose face scared Hitler into suicide, whose face fits perfectly in the shroud of Turin, whose face thrills women and men toward sacramental coitus, who profits from my coffee spills and correct *Jeopardy* answers. Andre we're on our way Andre. Andre the size model of condoms. Andre feet first to heaven. Omega.

POUNDED DOVER

And the ocean has a godly line this particular evening.
The waves break their hardest, the moon is spread eagle on the bed naked
Straddling the canal—on the beaches of Normandy the torch
Is like a supernova or a roman candle before it dies;
They say 'Cheerio' and offer tea from a ridiculous height,
With glitter and gaps, time swallows this monotonous gulf.
We're holding a boom-box outside your window!
We sugared the evening like you take it!
The ancient lineage of tumultuous waves.
The ocean mates a lunar lit landscape.
Ahoy! We hear the nails on the chalkboard like a lion's roar!
Sand newly liberated from the bondage of the breakers but freedom's brief
When it approaches the mighty belt,
Like a car's ignition sputters and starts on a cold morning,
A hesitant song is sung backwards, and delivers
One note on one bassoon held until the musician, weeping, draws in no air.

We heard the gossip on the Aegean, and we recalled the muddy vacillation
Of heavy sadness; we
Search for an un-inebriated prayer
Listening to the arctic like it's a radio program.
The ocean of believing's water almost drowned me
Near this beach
Lay like a belly's edge over too-tight pants.
We listen to the
Sad, endless, lionized back-stepping,
Beating off to the words of the breeze, and fall off
The bareback tiles of the globe

Oh, Arnold, let's be honest
With each other! This earth seems
Like an uneaten feast—
A rainbow, so like a goddess, but newborn,

Not by Aphrodite, Nor by Apollo, are we led.
Nothing is certain; life hurts. The shell is broken
Eternal nocturne, eternal Hades,
Blinded Mars called us by sirens to his bidding.
We war with the enemy by night, creating ...

II

ONE APE'S QUEST [1]

[1] Sonnets on 2–15 of this sequence take their titles from section titles in *The Gay Science* by Friedrich Nietzsche, edited by Bernard Williams and translated by Josefine Nauckhoff, Cambridge University Press, 2001.

1   Preface

My life has been a spinning wheel.
I rock less than I roll.
Whenever I try to stop and breathe
The hand reaches out and touches me
On the neck, tries to crush me.
The hand, the insidious hand,
Makes me avoid going outside.
And the hand, the insidious hand,
Breaks me back into a roll.
We'll all die
And where's my second lunch?
It's like that time we were given helium balloons
While in wretched captivity, took in their gas
When we talked the people just laughed!

2   Ideal and Material

The day after we were visited by man,
I took it upon myself to throw our ape medicine down the shithole.
As I addressed the crowd of follower chimps, I quoted myself,
"You envisage a noble ideal, but are *you* such a noble stone that such a divine
image could be fashioned out of you? And anyway—isn't all your work a
barbarous sculpting?
A blasphemy against your ideal?"
That was all they needed to hear on that matter.
We mated each other in the open air,
Flung our shit from the trees,
And laughed through our teeth.
I think I got some on my own mother's teat.
I presented my ass to my father with some extra sass
Just to prove the point
That to envy man is really to become him.

3   The Animal with a Good Conscience

We wear masks
On Monday through Friday from nine to five.
Wearing these masks is a very grim task.
That each mask is held on with tight tight glue.
Peeling it off each night is sometimes not even worth it.
And we've lost many comrades who have kept it on so long
That they forgot how to take it off.
And the only evidence is a deep red blush
Of their animal nature when confronted with their bodies' nature.
I wear my mask as a way of investigating the human task—
But not for more than three hours a day.
The glue I use decays quickly. Besides—I usually have to fart, cum,
Or make a call to Dionysus before lunch.
No one believes that I am Bismarck anyway...

4   The Animal with a Good Conscience / What We Should Be Grateful For

These humans I observe have phony manners in *their* masks.
They claim to enjoy such pleasures that strike my eardrums as all wrong.
Sitting at a desk or walking in uncomfortable shoes—
They claim these things will get them laid. But after all the work and delay,
Waiting in an airport while so many young Yves St. Laurent-wearing cunts
     walk by.
The only value is the artist and all men are artists.
Holding these raging pink "balloons" that say fuck me to a new pop
Tune. Who's got my needle? Who's got my thread? It doesn't matter who,
We're foreseeing ourselves dead!
The fun is in the artistry of beating off the unoriginal to wait for the clean.
I'm just sitting here in my tree watching you humans look foolish to me.
Look at my swelling! It's bulging and red!
That's all the apes here want to see. I have the most cred!

5   The Heaviest Weight

Hurrah! The demon came to me!
He said you fucking bastard, see!:
What's happening now forever will be!
I said what the fuck are you talking about, demon?!
I don't want a repeat of my dead-baby-eating!
It died most cruelly at the hands of an ex-lover!
I had to consume him! Hell—I am his mother!
The demon he answered with signature wit!
He said no one told you you had to eat *shit*!
I turned inward on myself and almost did cry!
But I am an ape! I don't look at the *sky*! I said "Hey demon, thanks for your time!
I won't be needing these," and gave him some wine!
His books, and his hat, and this messy thing *consciousness divine*!
Your ideas cannot crush me! I'm impenetrable to crime!

6   The Heaviest Weight

I licked a jar in the Congo,
And shaped it was, like my second bride, upon the plains.
What a smart civilized mess it made home look
Rhyming with my dinner plate.

The wilderness rose up to it,
My gang approached it after me,
We knocked it over, jumped on it, hoping there were bananas in it.
The jar was sweet broken shards on the grass.
And tall and farty wine mussed the air.
The jar was not allowed a thing.
We made more primate love everywhere. More monkey monkey love!
O Eternity, blind the sky from my eye
The jar did not heighten my struggle to escape or give me wild, wild ecstatic
    nights!
—Unlike everything else in the Congo.

7   Life Is a Disease

It has come to us from the lemurs, lower primates, who got this wretched
    syndrome
From lower mammals, who were given it from something with no hair,
Who got it from anything with more than one cell,
Who got it from a grain of sand. The only way to rid one's self of this evil is
    to end the evil.
Hand me that sword. Yes, you with five fingers on your paw! What? You
    can't pick it up?
Boo! Never mind. But the problem is that I cannot pick it up either. And
    without
More creative suicides, I am doomed to roam until I can pick up a quill to
    describe my agony,
Which is where we are now. I invite you, gentle reader, to take a hit:
    swallow this pill
Like Alice down the long shaft. I urge you, gentle reader, to go to the party
    because that's
The only place you'll meet death. And death is why you go to the party.
    When you arrive, look
Up at the thoughtfully arranged buntings. Look down at the cleanly swept
    floor for dancing,
And shake your bones. Don't be a whore. Shake. Let the E.T. finger
Dipped through the butt-shaped clouds touch your thumb.
Let there be life. And let yourself be liked. And no more.

8   The Agony of Knowing (An Ape's Reflection)

The heaviest weight is knowing.
The heaviest weight is knowing.
How many times have I said this to myself?
How many times have I said this to myself?
I looked at my reflection today and
I am hairier than I remembered being.
I couldn't make eye contact with myself.

It was straining.
I walked closer to the pool of water and threw a rock into it
To discourage my being.
It snapped back into me within seconds.
It is not a windy day and I am unchanged.
These are days to remember.
Denial is not borne only out of the great apes from the South.

9   Holy Cruelty

An ape we taught to look like a man became a priest for a bunch of humans.
He wore a foolish hat and we had to hold back our laughs
When he gave one man, a father, advice on being human.
From his beating big ape heart he said, "Kill your child right from the start!
Swaddle the body for three days, Christ, it softens your member!
And maybe you'll remember that human life is not to be trifled with!
Raising a sentient being carries severe weight. See: there is the knowing look
upon your face!" Exclaiming the Truth about your wretched race
And all the pains disguised by words like "martyrdom" and "grace,"
The priest he worked his Planet of the Charms.
A gong chimed truthfully when he explained from behind his knowing mask,
"It's crueler to let it live, and experience your (hiccough!) I mean our serious pain!
Hell, think of the pain you're feeling right now! Your mind spirals outward:
        it's no way to live! Hold funeral dirges for yourself. Start living to live!"

10   What We Should Be Grateful For

After the wise ape priest came down from his temple,
He peeled off his foolish hat and went to a museum,
Sang from his throat and beat off the whole way.
But when he reached the second floor of the Met,
His knuckles clanked to the floor and his jaw dropped, amazed.
The one art was not losing but finding that humans
Expressed their futures in such beautiful ways.

He wanted to be inside the paintings.
He wanted to scream that "Look they did it!"
The humans were on the stage once more.
Perhaps *that father* should ignore
Him. The human's true calling is mimicking reality
Like an ape on a joke kick. The human's true calling is art.
A religion can simply be a magnifying glass held at the right things.

11   Mothers

The law of the jungle indeed!
You humans I see have greatness achieved!
The women have played a holy-cruel joke!
It's good enough for a god with a heart condition to double over and croak!
Do you believe it?! The human women have achieved the impossible task!
They've made the men the workers! They barely pick up the slack!
Once they give birth, they lie on their backs! They're like the male lion!—
All headdress and crap! Just joking, I mean before a certain time!
Oh! I'd been looking through a cruel looking glass!
The women still run things from behind the scenes!
It pains you to hear Freddy scream!
Consciousness leads to thoughtful male mothers!
For the human mother is the horse and the carriage, and is rarely male!
The other problem is that "watching the game" *is productive!*

12   Learning to Pay Homage

Ahem, humans are stupid. See, when I praised my colleague following
The gorilla attack on our tribe in autumn 2005, I gave him my second wife
    to mate.
I never thought twice about it or tried to usurp his power aggressively or passively.
Our tribe depended upon his safety. If I were a human,
I would have created a TV parody, and perhaps a conspiracy theory to go
    along with it

About his power, undermining his well deserved success.

Humans use their energy misplacedly. I suppose I wouldn't mind if they were
funnier.

"Ahem." That is the sound of a human trying to accept his own failure that
someone has done

Exactly what he has wanted to do but failed. A chimp doesn't have these problems.

The mask, however transparent it is on him, however in line with his animal
sympathies,

Is still there. He will clear his throat, and that translates into "I have no
fucking clue

How to admit I'm in the red."

The Chimp is always in the red, and that is why He flashes you his backside.

It's the fu-fu-fucking rosemary for remembrance!

13   Origin of Knowledge

It's so funny how the humans create science labs

When they're the experiment themselves!

It's so funny to watch them try to "know" and make constant mistakes!

How ever does one evolve into this species called a "human being"?

The answer is by making a shitload of mistakes,

Like mating with the woman with the hairless body,

Moving too far north, where most human chimps are deaf to the sign

That it's teeth-chatteringly cold!

The humans and their "pursuit of knowledge": this houndstooth vest, a regress.

Have you seen "The Thinker" in their zooniversities? He has thought himself
out of a cave

And into a usefulness-free zone.

The Thinker looks so foolish with a furrow on his brow, sitting down.

Get him alone in a room with me and see what good his thinking does him.

Minus his arm, he won't be able to light his grand ol' pipe!

Hurrah! Hey Lefty, what is judgment, or ferment, or struggle, or this lust for
power tango?

14   The Hermit Speaks

We came upon a little shack where Goldilocks lives now. Attack her not—
We were delighted to find the secrets of her hermitage.
She feared our faces so we wore masks of Socrates, Nixon, and Gertrude Stein:
The ideal thinker, the crook, and a lover of good food.
Welcomed in, we took our place
Behind a mess of dinner plates.
And asked her using our hand signals,
Pant-hoots, and hollers of all shapes and sizes,
"Why have you left *your* civilization?"
She answered in English, "I'll tell you *sirs*:
There were three meals of man presented to me and none was to my fancy:
First, was I to swallow my courage, spend time with people who knew pretty
    much nothing?
Second, was I to flatter by stirring their idiocy into the stew of what I knew
    (a sin)?
Thirdly, I guess I wouldn't sink my teeth into something so boring my mind
    would scream!"

15   The Hermit Speaks Again

The masks: Are not just of Jordans! Or LeBrons! Or of ex-U.S. Presidents!
The masks: Are sometimes of ghosts from beyond!
The masks: Tremble me off, out of this whorehouse!
The masks: Open doors, especially when we're dead!
The masks: I'm impatient for my death!
The masks: Q: What were you thinking? A: I wanted to feel what muteness
    tastes like!
The masks: This loneliness is called life!
The masks: I speak posthumously!
The masks: I speak having made friends with my ghost!
The masks: Keep that chair propped up against the door to keep the humans out!
The masks: Don't let them blow it up!

The masks: I see a human wearing a Chimpanzee mask!
The masks: Our cover is blown! Quick! Hide!
The masks: Take your stinking paws off me! You damned dirty human! Die!

16

The hand reaches out and touches me
And laughed through our teeth.
I wear my mask as a way of investigating the human task—
The only value is the artist and all men are artists
I turned inward on myself and almost did cry!
What a smart civilized mess it made home look
Up at the thoughtfully arranged buntings. Look down at the cleanly swept
    floor for dancing,
It was straining.
From his beating big ape heart said, "Kill your child right from the start!"
The one art was not losing but finding that human
Consciousness leads to thoughtful male mothers.
The Chimp is always in the red, and that is why He flashes you his backside.
It's so funny to watch them try to "know" and make constant mistakes!
She feared our faces so we wore masks of Socrates, Nixon, and Gertrude Stein.
The masks: I speak posthumously!

III

LAW

Keep raining.
Hoard your principles.
Abide the rules for years to come.
Buy crackers weeks and weeks ahead.
The test, postponed, is ten years long anyway.
A man long ago crapped on a redacted etiquette book
Established by dandies and kept by law.
The only wig to wear was the only way to shine.
Due to the opening of the box,
Perhaps by stealing so much cash,
Abiding or not, the designation stayed.

Our people fell back into shade.
We took the apple, bit it hard,
Sewed the seed into the sand,
The deserts, rainbows, and the grass:
Where all our growing now stands tall.

Concrete or supple, my breast is bared.
Who among you is an areola-sharer?
A camera trembles around my neck
Chronicling many past immortal days.
And still the test continues in this way.
My mouth drips with another's spit.
I search for a redeeming blanked face
Among those playing Nero in the rain.
But I am running for the lowest office.
Lore told me cameras on strings can tremble one sane.
My hair is back to its length before the flood,
Before the riot in the garden has ruptured.
The law is never wrong. That's what law is.

PROWLING

Dried relatives under land (our land).
Properly waked,
We return to them.
We somehow always return
To the idea of zero.
Wearing a suit and clean underwear,
Swearing underground
In a soundproof box.
We're a stable packed with sages
Who bite down on
Hay fed to us so we shut up.
Wearing a mustard suit with a matching noose,
Under all this latex and wax—
Does this bullet hole make my butt look big?
Blood got on all my paperwork my magazines my satin insides.
My will was explicit: no diapers.
My will was explicit: fill me with solid cotton.
I am not wearing cowboy boots or buckled shoes in my coffin.
I don't need to.
I float.
I'm all thrust.
We Americans we float like angels or like witches.
My halo, my charmed halo my feet a few feet above water—
Catch me if you can.
No reflection of me in the mailbox or the mirror or the . . .
I'm visible only in parking lot oil puddles or TV screens and
I've clearly been working out.
My halo flickers fluorescent
Before it runs out of light.
I borrowed some matches
These lights stay out.
Night
Arid, starless, new moon.

JUST ANOTHER GOAT SONG

I'm turning the spit for Dionysus
Lighting the pan drips for Dionysus
I'm carefully staying in character
So things don't get funny around here
Happy families are all the same
But we're poking out of this trash bag from every direction
Someone didn't buy Glad this year
Leaving no ventilation for improv
Just please *try* to climax *in your bed* in Act III
And die on the last page of Act V
And if you don't die on the last page of Act V
Please ask your ghost or a close friend to explain
Amor fati in your stead

BLEATING HEART

Her bust is sliced once in the middle despite her dignity.
Glory.
Like dessert.
And he waited, a hungry goat.

See you later, she says.

He answers her with these words:
Oh, please stop by the Acropolis later.
Farmers and families will be hanging out.
It would be great to see you.

But I was at the delta all day waiting for you, she says.

He chews on this atop his rock,
Pictures a nativity and smiles.

He did not know he was inviting her to his own sacrifice.

To Ganymede, Before Your Move To Mount Olympus

Pack some liquor and an aerobics video
Because you'll be penned up like veal and carted
From one old person's house to another, but in the clouds.

Leave it to Hera to help you with your bags.
She'll drop them doggedly, exposing her nips and
Your nips of peach-flavored vodka.

Zeus will give you some menial job to justify your presence.
He'll ask you to bend over to pick up objects
He has spells to lift on his own.

I keep thinking your ride should have picked you up by now.
Zeus drives a midlife crisis balding eagle nowadays.
Make sure to go to the bathroom. It's a long flight.

BAKER'S DAUGHTER

"They say the owl was a baker's daughter. Lord, we know what we are, but know not what we may be." Ophelia, *Hamlet*

No! I am not Ophelia.

O yeah, I lay with a crazy
But it was just for one night

Among him as his own
To sing a boding song, wave a tender bone.

I fed the meter, built a bridge,
Grabbed a honey, pumped the midg'.

Alack, the smack of truth.

The prince did insert his fangs into my back
And then, ok, ok, you were right!
It all went black!

But tremble I did not. My father lives
Don't have a brother and I never will
Let my flesh stink to high heaven
Cover it with a wreath homemade
And expect it to do the job of Glade

FINDING A CURE FOR BEING HUMAN

I

The man who executive produces
Expensive movies that exploit our fears:

Of terrorists (death by a jetliner wearing a towel)
Of aliens (death by a UFO wearing a towel), or
Of natural disasters (a cloud wearing a towel),
Of murder most foul (a man not wearing a towel suddenly finding himself
    wearing a towel).
The kind of person whose testicles are their own religion; bow to them.
The kind of person who stays up all night because she's afraid of the day ending.
For every minute you avoid shit, a stadium fills up with diarrhea.
For every minute you're not in France, you're arrested.
For every minute you wipe your ass, that's one swipe against mankind.

The six year old I was, holding a fake gun, despising the loud, the drunk.
The six year old I was, holding the fake gun, calling my big sister a *fucking bastard*.
The six year old I will always be, middle child, my family faking right.

A monster who has lived as long as you, but has never been to Greece.
A monster who can read, but has no concept of current events.
A monster who can walk for miles, but swears he's innocent.
A monster on fire, breathing heavy, is a broken dream.

II

Watch this video of a parrot raping another parrot.
Everyone knows parrots learn all they know from their humans,
Which means this parrot's owner raped a parrot.
My species is so goddamned sick.

III

Possible Solutions:

1. A self-portrait as an Asian baby.
2. A self-portrait as a corpse years from now (silicone and hair but no skin).
3. A self-portrait thirty years from now, long divorced, my organs already decaying, my DNA strands occasionally fucking up the replication cycle for new layers of skin, liver cells, and uterine tissue leading to certain cancer.

IV

Caesar Augustus
Had one daughter
Named Julia
Who loved fucking so much
He sent her into exile.
The love a father can pour so easily into one jar,
As into the next.

Every pair of pants
Gets a bulge sometime, betraying some
Tacit guile.
When really, Julia had lost her youthful glow
And no one really wanted to see *that*.

ORANGE JULIUS

But for these pigeons,
we'd be living the high life.
Mucking about
Rome, I'm dying, you're all dying.
We're all dying.
Capture my heart.
In the words of *me*,
and you and you and you and you and you and you, and you Brutus?
Preserve the republic.

But for these pigeons,
we'd be living the high life.
Deeply in debt,
I signed up to conquer Gaul,
sent letters
came saw conquered
preferred my image
in the mirror
to that of anyone else.

Played hours of heads or tails with my own face.

Just last night,
I saw a deer
outside my window.
Scared the shit out of me so bad
I had to stutter
the evening's official pronouncement
while pissing in the backyard
while Julia and Julia Junior and Julia Junior Junior did their hair:
You ca-ca-can take the boy out of nature.
But you can't ta-ta-take nature
out of the b-b-b-b-b-b-boy.

CARPE DIE

I

Shut the door. Did anyone recognize you?
Indecent vitamins and sandy morning nostrils
We had each other for breakfast

Spread-eagle bed, American fucking
Fucking an eagle makes me feel like a fundamentalist beast
Tax evaders buttfuck eagle in their sleep

II

I enjoyed being Caesar
The birth
The dressing
The embarrassment and the humiliation
having a particularly large head for my age

Bobby, don't listen to me
I hated my birth
I hated my death
Blood and blood
It's been a red life

III

A man opens a letter
A ghost approaches with a chainsaw demanding postage from the grave
The man with the letter running and reading
And tripping he cries and holds his leg
The ghost grabs the leg and cuts off thirty-nine cents worth

Now pedicured, he reads the letter:

Dear Bobby,

Exterior of a Japanese park
Carps gorged out on food lie enraptured
Having each come on its own vomit
One white carp wakes up horny
Sees a red orange carp through the murky water
He twists upright and drunk takes three right corners to get to her
He nuzzles up to her mouth and they kiss bubbles to each other
The bubbles reach the surface of the pond.

A worm covered in a red powdered hallucinogenic aphrodisiac descends
Carps pounce on it like great dane cock to poodle pussy
A boy lifts the horny carps into his bucket
White carp spewing around bucket like filthy porn
And they sputter off their life gorged on each other

Lost breath
We all tasted metal
And we're sad again

Sincerely,
Caesar

IV

In the forests I humped the air wishing for architecture
I rubbed the air again to feel the cavern between my thighs
I climbed the three mountains

Going nuts never stayed me from deforestation
As a nymph still chilled by the chance of degradation

Who's that at the door? It's Bobby and he's back for more
He wants to eat mescaline and make love on the carpet
How do you say get the fuck away from me in Italian?

Acknowledgements

Some of these poems appeared previously in the following: *Canon Magazine*, *Red China Magazine*, *The Dick Pig Review*, *Agriculture Reader*, *HungryHungryHipster.com*, and *Sub-Lit*. "Finding a Cure for Being Human" and "Flaming O" first appeared in the chapbooks *Baby Suri and the Sea Otter, A Dialogue: Exploring Identity in the Modern World* and *Corey Feldman and the Flamingo, A Dialogue: The Struggles of an Icon*, respectively. They were written with Maggie Wells and published by Press Body Press.

Thanks to my family and friends, and special thanks to Maggie Wells, Paul Violi, Michael McDonough, Liesel Tarquini, Alex Smith, and Eleanor Jaekel.

AMY LAWLESS holds her MFA from the New School. She is the co-founder of Press Body Press and a contributing editor to the *Dick Pig Review*. She was born in Boston and lives in Brooklyn, New York.

Black Maze Books will publish a shortlist of talented artists and writers over the next several years. We will print both emerging artists and those established in their fields, and promote other projects in the world of arts and letters. BMB publishes a limited run of each book, but remains on-demand through Lulu.com and by extension other on-line and brick-and-mortar booksellers who support us. For a full list of our books, bookseller partners, and other contributors, please visit us on the web at: blackmazebooks.com.

Noctis Licentia was designed by Eleanor Jaekel. It is set in Gcudy Old Style type.

www.ingramcontent.com/pod-product-compliance
Lightning Source LLC
Chambersburg PA
CBHW031525040426
42445CB00009B/405